Solving the Discipline Puzzle

Understanding Instructional Discipline

Tricia Wells

ISBN # 0-9716304-0-2

© Copyright 2001
All Rights Reserved.

Printed in the United States of America.
Cover Art: Todd Pierce

Published and Distributed by:

Longmont, CO • (303) 776-2083
www.creatingstudentsuccess.com

Table of Contents

Preface 1

1. What Do We Know?
The Child at the Schoolhouse Door 3
The Traditional View of Discipline 5
Faulty Assumptions of Discipline 6
The Instructional View of Discipline 7
Common Concerns 10

2. What Do We Believe?
Beliefs About Behavior and Discipline 13
Beliefs About Change and School Improvement 16

3. What Do We Want To Achieve?
Schoolwide Discipline 19
    Clear Expectations 19
    Preventive Teaching 20
    High Staff Visibility and Supervision 21
    Frequent Feedback 21
    Positive Relationships 22
Individual Student Support 23
    Support for Classroom Disruptions 23
    Team-based Planning and Problem Solving 25
    Individual Behavior Plans 25
    School, Home and Community Collaboration 25

4. How Do We Achieve the Vision?
Positive and Proactive Philosophy 27
Ongoing School Improvement 27
Determining Readiness 30
School Profile 30

References 35

Visuals

Figure 1 *Academic & Social Problems: A Comparison of Approaches* 9

Figure 2 *Punishment vs. Discipline* 12

Figure 3 *Beliefs for a New View of Discipline* 18

Figure 4 *Continuum of Behavior Support* 24

Figure 5 *Instructional Discipline* 26

Figure 6 *The Ongoing Discipline Process* 29

"Our children are the living message we send to a time we will not see."
– Neil Postman

Preface

The above quote reflects my unrelenting commitment to our youth today, especially those who are troubled or troublesome by virtue of their behavior. As a nation, we look to our schools to prepare our young people with the skills necessary for a successful and productive adulthood. This expectation is characteristically addressed in school mission statements that, with few variations, avow, "to provide educational opportunities that enable all students to achieve to their fullest potential." Whether or not students develop the competencies necessary for this success in life depends, at least in part, on our ability to ensure school cultures and climates that promote not only academic success, but also social, emotional, and behavioral success in a disciplined learning environment.

After almost thirty years of classroom teaching, consulting with and supervising teachers, and serving as an administrator or a staff developer in residential, clinical and public school settings, there is one thing of which I am certain—schools cannot achieve high academic outcomes for their children without attending to school climate and discipline. Goodlad (1984), following his extensive review of successful schools states, "Schools differed in their ability to create academic success, but the differences appear to be more related to school and classroom climate factors than to methods of teaching. Successful schools paid more than average attention to the quality of interactions among those inhabiting the school and to the social context in which those interactions occur." Only when schools create a climate of respect, responsibility and self-discipline can learning flourish.

In the face of this simple truth, I am also keenly aware that schools today are confronted with contemporary challenges not faced by educators before. Every year, schools are being asked to do more with fewer resources. A critical public and state and federal governments have demanded initiatives to improve literacy, character, technology, school safety, etc. Expectations to address these new initiatives unfortunately do not come with permission to cease work on others.

Educators are also expected to teach an increasingly heterogeneous group of students with significant learning and/or behavioral problems. The number of students with disabilities served under IDEA continues to grow at a greater rate than the population and school enrollment. Over the past ten years, these students are being served in classrooms with non-disabled peers more and more. Many of these are students with intense behaviors that require comprehensive behavioral support.

The result of these challenges is a growing sense of frustration and feelings of failure, not only for our students, but also for school personnel. However, the problem is not the lack of effective procedures and practices. A growing body of evidence over the past twenty years supports practical interventions for preventing and reducing behavior problems. Gathered from research on effective schools, applied behavioral analysis, and social learning theory, these approaches are being encouraged through the efforts of the Center on Positive Behavior Supports and the U.S. Department of Education's Offices of Special Education Programs and Safe and Drug-Free Schools.

These research-based practices offer much promise, yet schools have had great difficulty in establishing these practices into their daily operations. The answer lies in a systemic approach to change that focuses on creating collaborative school improvement processes to effectively utilize these evidence-based practices.

Extending the focus of our schools from solely academic success to include social success does not entail lengthening the school day, eliminating existing coursework, or extending graduation requirements. It should not mean additional work for educators. Rather it requires working smarter. It requires the dedication of staff to unify and create structures and routines that address social behavior as an ongoing part of the school curriculum in all classrooms, corridors, playgrounds, and office areas each and every day. It requires us to use time more efficiently and strategically by selecting approaches that have proven effectiveness.

Such dedication to student social success obviously requires that teachers and administrators be provided with the principles and practical strategies to guide their change efforts. These materials are dedicated to assist educators in making the lasting changes that will meet the social, emotional and behavioral needs of *all* children.

What Do We Know?

Education should not and cannot be for the select few who come to school from environments that helped them become not only academically inclined but also socially acceptable to peers and adults.

While a high level of academic achievement remains a primary goal of education, there can be little disagreement that student social, emotional and behavioral problems often impede that goal. For more than twenty-five years, the *Annual Gallup Poll of the Public's Attitudes Toward the Public Schools* identified "lack of discipline" as the most serious problem facing our educational system. Sixty percent of new teachers leave the profession within their first five years, often citing poor student discipline as the cause.

National dialogue continues among school personnel and parents calling for solutions to the increasing incidence of insubordination, truancy, drug use, and intimidation that lead to the more than two million suspensions each year. For the twenty percent of our students who do not complete school, these dropouts have been linked to behavioral issues such as social skills deficits, suspensions, and feelings of disconnectedness (Gresham, 1981; Wagner, 1991). In addition, classrooms are plagued by other more minor misbehaviors that, while they do not result in suspension, disrupt learning. Research shows that approximately one-half of classroom time is taken up with non-instructional activities, and discipline problems are responsible for a significant portion of this lost instructional time (Cotton, 1990).

The Child at the Schoolhouse Door

There is a common perception that more students are coming to school today lacking the self-discipline, respect, responsibility, character, and interpersonal skills necessary for school success. While this increase in student discipline problems may be partially attributed to the fact that we are educating more of our youth today than any time in history, societal trends also present us with a different and often challenging child at the schoolhouse door.

Poverty. In 1998 over 21% of our children lived in poverty; one out of every four children under age 6 were living in poverty. For African-American children this figure is 40%, and for Latinos, 32%. In high poverty neighborhoods, 20% of 16- to 19-year olds are high school dropouts. One out of every three children live in single parent homes and experience the diminished economic and human resources linked to these households.

Drug Use. Nationally twenty percent of our youth above the age of 12 claim to have used illicit drugs. While often associated with large urban districts with diverse populations, rural areas have not been immune to the effects of youth drug abuse and the related violence and breaches of security.

Diminished Supervision. Parental supervision is down 40-50% from the early 1970's. Today, ninety percent of families in the United States either are headed by a single parent or have both parents working outside the home. Other studies indicate that many parents spend less than ten minutes per day interacting with their children. Single parents and working families often do not have the time to teach their children responsibility, supervise them and provide the necessary guidance and feedback. As a result, many of our children spend much of their time in unsupervised environments, fending for themselves, and learning how to behave from questionable sources such as television and their peers (Crews, 1997). In fact, research tells us that for many of our children today, television and their peers are the number one and two long-term influences on their lives.

> A good portion of our children today spend much of their time in unsupervised environments, learning from potentially undesirable sources.

One might expect that many of these infrequent adult-child interactions occur as reactions to problems. As parents spend less time with their children, expectations are likely to be unclear. When misbehavior occurs, these parents may be quick to anger, yell or punish. It is not difficult to understand why parents and educators alike report a growing number of youth who are unresponsive to their interactions, direction and guidance, and easily become angry, defensive or argumentative when engaged by an adult.

Diminished Respect for Role-bound Authority. Perhaps there was a time when the legitimate authority of teachers, principals and parents was so strong that discipline problems were minimized, but it can no longer be taken for granted that learners will come to school with inherent respect for teachers' authority. Some teachers claim that the seriousness of discipline problems today is directly related to this erosion of role-bound authority. Most have heard student challenges such as, *"You can't make me!"* or *"I don't have to do what you say!"* Similar disrespect occurs with police and other authorities, and students today clearly feel that they are equals with adults or, in some cases, above all authority.

Higher Incentives for Negative Behavior. Too many of our youth no longer want to be "good." News media heralds the anti-hero and children's shows glamorize the anti-authority protagonist. Television and movies portray young people who follow rules, work hard, are dependable and responsible as nerds, dweebs, geeks or other current terms of derision, while portraying "powerful" youth as rude, hostile, devious and manipulative, who never get caught or held accountable. Negative behavior appears to offer youth increased importance with peers and even perceived financial gain.

Increased Exposure to Violence. Some children have become insensitive to violence, accepting it as a normal way of life. By adolescence, the average child has witnessed 18,000 acts of violence. We live in a society where shootings, knifings and fistfights are commonplace. For some students a physical response to life's problems is all that they comprehend, and non-violent skills for disagreeing, negotiating, or problem solving are unknown.

"Me" Generation. Societal trends in parenting have also produced over-indulged children. These children have been placed at the center of attention and protected from failure, frustration or disappointment by parents who cater to all their children's wants including to be entertained, receive special treatment, to have easy success, acceptance of inappropriate behavior, and even control over adults. These parents give them permission to do almost anything they want and allow them to act in a disrespectful and irresponsible manner. Overindulged students have not learned to take responsibility for their actions, to do without, to delay gratification, or the importance of developing the interpersonal skills necessary to acquire the respect and things they want.

Limited Value for Education. For some of our students the role of a learner, the learning process, and the value of an education are vague at best. School is all too often merely the place they go each day while their parents are off to other activities. For others, school was not a successful experience for their parents and that negative view has been passed on. Educators are discovering that many motivation, achievement, and behavior problems are the result of students not understanding their *role* as a learner, *how* to learn and *why* (Jones, 1995).

Loss of Relational Security. Some children come to school today with unmet basic security needs. We have become a "throw away" society where we casually discard husbands, wives, children and things. Children may be shuffled around to various relatives for care and subsequently to different schools. This message of expendability often continues into our schools where exclusionary discipline practices threaten to callously eliminate students who do not or cannot behave. These children feel they do not have relationships that include a personal commitment to their long-term development.

> Whether neglected or over-indulged, the results are the same–more students are coming to school without the self-discipline, respect, responsibility and social skills needed to be successful.

While students today may be different, our approaches to discipline have not changed. If we are to be successful, we must rethink our approaches to student discipline and our commitment to helping each child achieve, not only academically, but also socially (Walker et al, 1996).

The Traditional View of Discipline

For the most part our approaches to school discipline are still based on punitive and exclusionary policies developed in the early 1900s when schools were oriented toward the academically inclined and socially acceptable. In the agrarian society of that time, success in school was not a prerequisite to getting a job. The goal was not to educate all, and schools graduated only 6% of the population. It was not until the 1940s that schools graduated 50% of our students and since the 1960s that 75% or more of the population completed school.

Whether intentionally or unintentionally, schools historically have been exclusive. Discipline policies acted as a means to weed out students less able, less motivated, or poorly behaved. But times have changed. Without a high school education today, prospects for life success are very poor. Schools can no longer function as exclusive systems. We must ensure life preparedness—academic and social—for all.

Though times have changed, our beliefs about student misbehavior and the discipline policies we use have not. When educators are asked to define *discipline* the most common response is "punishment for rule-breaking behavior" (USA Today, 1991). Administrators and teachers talk of lists of prohibitive rules and a series of increasingly severe punishments for the violators of these rules. Unfortunately, such a punitive view of discipline results in approaches that have questionable if not harmful effects. Punishment focuses on what not to do, does not teach the desired behaviors, can damage relationships and impede learning (Mayer & Sulzer-Azeroff, 1991). Punishment typically includes exclusionary practices such as detentions, in-school suspension, homebound instruction, shortened school day, referral to alternative schools, administrative transfers, or ignored truancies that restrict student access and learning.

Some administrators and teachers feel that punitive and exclusionary policies are fine and have served us well. They view discipline activities as irritating and unnecessary intrusions into their teaching agendas. Use of them continues because of the immediate and seemingly positive effects offered by the short-term solution of removing the problem students. Older students with more serious behavioral difficulties often drop out, as school administrators fail to create successful alternatives. Unfortunately, these outcomes are in direct conflict with school missions to help all students achieve their fullest potential (Walker, Colvin, & Ramsey, 1995).

Faulty Assumptions of Traditional Discipline

The punitive and exclusionary policies of the past fail today partly because they are based on some faulty assumptions. First, punitive approaches assume that students *know* the right way to behave, that their misbehavior is a *performance deficit* and that they have the skills but are merely choosing defiance or insubordination. We therefore assume that punishment will bring a halt to the inappropriate behavior and the student will instead behave appropriately.

The unfortunate reality is that often the child at the schoolhouse door today does not know how to behave in socially acceptable ways. The high probability explanation for many discipline problems today is *skill deficit*—the child has a limited repertoire of behaviors and does not know how to behave responsibly. As shared before, some come from homes where parental guidance is limited or absent, others from homes that model ineffective problem-solving or disrespectful and hostile interactions. Blaming the child and responding by "getting tough" will not alter this skill deficit.

Faulty Assumptions About Discipline

1. *Students know the right way to behave and are merely choosing to be defiant or insubordinate.*

2. *At risk students have a strong desire to be in school; the threat of exclusion deters misbehavior.*

3. *Discipline and punishment are the same thing. Students will not behave unless we "get tough."*

We must not use discipline policies that discriminate against students who come from homes that cannot, do not know how, or do not care to prepare their children with the behavioral repertoires that support education. Do we punish students for their disadvantage? Or do we teach the disrespectful student to be respectful, the unmotivated student to be motivated, the irresponsible student to be responsible?

Secondly, discipline policies that rely on exclusion fail the very students they target by assuming that these students have a strong desire to be in school. The threat of suspension or expulsion only works as a deterrent to misbehavior with students who value education, know how to be a responsible student, and want to be in school. This is not a reasonable assumption for at-risk students who feel little connection to school and routinely experience academic failure and social disapproval. Is it reasonable to exclude students with social, emotional, and behavioral needs from the one environment that may allow them to learn the value of an education and the vital skills, behaviors, and attitudes necessary to function successfully, not only in school, but in the community and later on the job?

Finally, many feel that maintaining high standards for behavior and low or "zero" tolerances for misbehavior requires getting tough—that the solution to discipline problems rests solely in finding a "bigger club." This limited view mistakes upholding standards with punishment—inflicting pain or penalty for an offense. No amount of punishment will bring about change in behavior if students do not understand and possess a full repertoire of responsible behaviors.

Recent studies show that an overemphasis on punishment focuses the students' attention on the negative consequences and limits thoughtful consideration of either the effect their behavior has on others or the long-term outcomes associated with continuing the behavior. Use of increasingly harsh punishment may actually lead to anti-social behavior (Mayer & Sulzer-Azeroff, 1991). This punishment orientation reinforces a low level of moral development and does not help students develop a higher, more socially valuable code of behavior. It fails to recognize that maintaining high standards is more a function of clarifying, teaching, supervising and providing students with feedback about their behavior. High standards and low tolerances are not synonymous with punishment.

Instructional View of Discipline

> dis•ci•pline n. (fr. Latin *disciplina,* teaching, learning) Instruction that corrects, molds or perfects character and develops self-control.
>
> Webster's New Collegiate Dictionary

As we seek to develop a more inclusive educational system, our attitudes regarding discipline must change. Is *discipline* concerned with punishing misconduct or with preventing it? According to the dictionary, it refers to prevention and remediation, "training to act in accordance with rules;" and "instruction and exercise designed to train to proper conduct or action" (*American College Dictionary);* "training that is expected to produce a specified character or pattern of behavior;" and "controlled behavior resulting from such training" (*American Heritage Dictionary).* Not until the third defi-

What Do We Know?

nition is there reference to punishment—"punishment intended to correct or train." The primary focus of discipline is training, instruction, and teaching. Discipline is the slow, bit-by-bit, sometimes time-consuming task of helping students to see the sense of acting in certain ways. Yet, many discipline policies are merely a collection of punishments to hopefully suppress behavior problems. Clearly, schools spend too much time attempting to eliminate inappropriate behavior rather than to teach and accelerate responsible behavior.

> "There are those who would admonish their pupils 'to behave' rather than teach them how to relate positively to each other. Seldom would we admonish a pupil to read in place of teaching the necessary skills."
>
> Morse, 1982

Reaching today's students requires an "instructional" approach to discipline with a focus on teaching—teaching students to be successful and behave responsibly in school. This instructional view of discipline is based on the belief that social behavior is learned and therefore can be taught. Students can be taught socially acceptable ways of behaving just as one would teach any other academic subject. When teaching a new math or reading skill, students are carefully instructed, opportunities to practice are provided, and encouragement and correction offered until students reach mastery. When academic errors occur, teachers typically respond with corrective teaching. Students are making social errors every day; why would we respond to social errors with punishment?

Discipline should be based on the very same instructional concepts used to facilitate academic learning. Direct instruction in effective social behaviors can be provided to students, and practice, encouragement, and correction can be given as needed. And just as with academics, when behavior problems are complex or chronic, specialized interventions or intensive teaching arrangements may be necessary. A comparison of approaches to academic and social problems is outlined in Figure 1.

> "Social skills should be taught to children using the same strategies that are used to teach academic skills—direct instruction, practice, and feedback."
>
> Colvin & Sugai, 1988

Central to this instructional approach is the ability to view misbehavior as a teaching opportunity. When discipline problems occur, educators are given an opportunity to address the skill deficits by teaching alternative behaviors that are more appropriate. This is the "teachable moment." When social errors occur, the learning is relevant and students are actively involved. When misbehavior occurs, instead of asking, *"How can we nail these kids harder?"* the question should be, *"How can we teach them better?"* or, what interventions can we use to help students learn to behave responsibly?

> "When it comes to discipline, it does not make sense for educators to use the criminal justice model first, before employing what they were professionally prepared to use—teaching and mentoring approaches."
>
> Forest Gathercoal, 1993

This understanding of the instructional role of discipline allows administrators and teachers to be proactive and remain objective in the face of problem behavior, to focus on teaching out of care and concern for students rather than react angrily, personally, defensively, or punitively. An instructional discipline policy moves staff away from the punitive or exclusionary practices of the past. The goal becomes teaching and maintaining high standards for responsible student behavior and keeping all students in school where they can continue to learn and grow both academically and behaviorally. Only then can schools fulfill their missions of helping students achieve their fullest potential. Some of the differences between the traditional, more punitive approach to discipline and an instructional view are summarized in Figure 2 on page 12.

Academic & Social Problems: *A Comparison of Approaches*[1]

Error Type	Approaches for *Academic Problems*	Misguided Approaches for *Social Problems*
Infrequent	Assume student is trying to make correct response; error was accidental, a *skill deficit*. Provide assistance *(teach, model, guide, check)*. Provide more practice and feedback; monitor progress. Assume student has learned skill and will perform correctly in the future.	Assume student is choosing to be "bad;" error was deliberate, a *performance deficit*. Provide negative consequence. Practice not required. Assume student "learned" lesson and will behave in the future.
Frequent	Assume student has learned the wrong way or has inadvertently been taught wrong way. Diagnose problem; identify misrule or determine more effective way to teach. Adjust teaching arrangements to accommodate learner needs. Provide practice and feedback Assume student has been taught skill and will perform correctly in the future.	Assume student is refusing to cooperate; student *knows* what is right, has been told to stop, and is being *insubordinate*. Provide more severe negative consequences; remove student from normal context *(office referral, detention, suspension, etc.)* Maintain student removal from the normal context. Assume student has "learned" lesson and will behave in the future.

[1] Adapted from Colvin & Sugai, 1988.

Figure 1

Common Concerns

When it comes to student behavior, schools everywhere are more alike than different. Focus groups, staff surveys, and conversations with building administrators, teachers, and paraeducators all reflect a common uneasiness and similar concerns. These concerns can be grouped into three categories: 1) limited knowledge and skills, 2) ineffective school improvement processes, and 3) confusing policies or procedures.

Knowledge and Skills. Most educators agree that they are not adequately prepared with the skills needed to effectively deal with today's discipline problems. Others feel that while they may have the tools, there is not a framework for consistent implementation of known best practices across their building staff. Most principals admit that administrative coursework did not cover how to effectively handle discipline referrals. Some of the knowledge and skills concerns include:

- Many staff still hold firmly to punitive and reactive discipline practices and believe that finding "a bigger club" is the solution to current problems.

- Most school discipline plans are based on a collection of prohibitive behaviors or rules and corresponding consequences that perpetuate a focus on "policing" or catching students who violate these rules.

- Staff responses to misbehavior are individual and reflect disparate tolerance levels, resulting in confusing and conflicting messages being sent to students and parents.

- Teachers lack a broad range of responses for routine discipline problems to maintain the integrity of the learning environment, and often resort to exclusionary practices and unnecessary discipline referrals.

- Many teachers need assistance to structure their classrooms for success—to teach classroom procedures and routines, build positive relationships and prevent discipline problems.

- Administrators are troubled by the widely variable use of office referrals. Some staff refer students excessively or unnecessarily while others allow problem behaviors to continue, disrupting the learning of all.

- Educators may distribute discipline handbooks or briefly review rules, assuming that students can be expected to behave accordingly. An understanding of the teaching role of discipline is lacking.

- At-risk students often become disruptive or fail before assistance with planning or developing interventions is initiated.

- School staff are discouraged with the increasing severity of discipline problems and seek strategies to work with chronic or intense student behaviors.

- Difficult parents often contribute to discipline problems, obstructing the development and implementation of possible solutions. Teachers are asking for help to successfully engage parents.

School Improvement Processes. Discipline is a process not a product or mere collection of strategies. Many schools experience roadblocks to their change efforts because of ineffectual processes:

- Many schools lack the leadership (i.e., administrator commitment or instructional leaders) necessary to establish the vision, plan and conduct development activities, and implement and monitor discipline practices in an ongoing way.

- "One shot" inservices have served to merely increase awareness and the level of staff concern but have not resulted in substantial improvement in practices.

- Similarly, isolated training of individuals or small groups from a building often does not lead to building-wide implementation.

- Some schools have focused on the completion of a written school policy. The policy, written by a few, has not led to "buy in" and consistent implementation by all.

- Recently hired teachers have missed the initial training activities and do not receive the support needed to develop successful discipline practices. Overtime, discipline procedures fade or change.

- Staff development activities have often overlooked those who may need the training the most (e.g., bus drivers, paraprofessionals, etc.)

Policies and Procedures. Schools also acknowledge that policies and procedures, or often the absence of these, impede their discipline efforts. These issues include:

- Schools often lack highly skilled staff that can provide assistance with functional assessments and the development of specialized behavioral supports.

- Problem solving teams are overwhelmed or do not know how to work efficiently to provide support for students before they fail.

- Schools lack creative alternatives to exclusionary practices such as detentions, in-school and out-of-school suspensions, etc.

- Formal structures for schools to interface efficiently and effectively with parents, the police, courts, juvenile authorities, and other community agencies are absent.

- Current discipline procedures for special education students often result in dual policies and confusion.

Schools everywhere are looking for practical solutions to these and other similar concerns.

Punishment vs. Discipline

Punishment	Instructional Discipline
• Seeks to inflict *pain or penalty* for an offense.	• Seeks to *train for correction* and maturity; self-discipline.
• Something *hurtful* must happen.	• Something *instructional* must happen.
• Concerned about *past misdeeds*; seeks a short-term solution.	• Concerned about *future correct deeds*; seeks a long-term solution.
• Focuses on the *problem behavior*.	• Focuses on the *desired behavior*.
• Adult attitude of *hostility and anger*.	• Adult attitude of *care and concern*.
• Emphasizes rules and immediate *negative consequences*.	• Emphasizes the *effects* the behavior has on self and others.
• Works only if the student is "*afraid*."	• Ensures an *emotionally safe* environment.
• Damages relationships; student *resents* punisher.	• Builds relationships; student *respects* adult.
• Student feelings of *fear, guilt, failure, resentment or anger*.	• Student feelings of *stability*.
• Student is *hurt*.	• Student is *strengthened*.
• Reinforces the child's failure identity and *poor self-concept*.	• Strengthens child's *self-concept*, builds *self-respect*.
• *External* locus of control.	• *Internal* locus of control or self-control.
• Often *removes* the child from school.	• *Maintains* the child in the learning environment.
• Threatens to *terminate relationship* with child.	• Strengthens *relational security*.

Figure 2

What Do We Believe?

Any school improvement effort begins with determining what you really care about and want to accomplish and then committing yourself to it. You can always develop expertise. First you must discover your beliefs.

With the recognition of a need to change our approaches to discipline, old attitudes or premises must give way to new ones. Our beliefs about student behavior and discipline unify us and guide our actions–the decisions we make, the practices we choose, and our interactions with others. The following beliefs reflect current literature and best practices and personal experiences with many schools across the country as they have undertaken discipline initiatives.

Beliefs About Behavior and Discipline

▶ *Education today must include a balanced focus on both academic achievement and social competency.*

As early as 1971, G. D. Borich advanced the position that social development has more impact than cognitive development on determining success or failure in school as well as society. In 1996, the Alliance for Curriculum Reform set forth new goals for student learning in the 21st century which included: 1) learning to learn and integrating knowledge, 2) communication skills, 3) thinking and reasoning, 4) interpersonal skills, and 5) personal and social responsibility. This emphasis on social competence by the schools is resounded by the world of work. A lack of interpersonal skills has been linked to juvenile delinquency, grade retention, suspensions, truancy, dropping out, lower self-esteem, and delayed cognitive development. As adults, social deficits have been correlated with inability to gain and maintain employment, discharge from military service, involvement with the judicial system, and mental health problems (Gresham, 1981).

To be successful today, students must understand their role and responsibilities as learners and possess a full repertoire of social skills that empower them to interact responsibly with adults and peers, not only in school, but at home, in the community, and eventually on the job. Since social competence plays such a significant role in life-long success, it is a legitimate school task worthy of our time and resources.

▶ *Increasing behavioral concerns require building-wide, systematic and proactive approaches.*

Few would disagree that school is the primary place where socialization occurs for children. Yet, historically schools have not addressed this critical function directly or systematically, and there is little evidence to suggest that personal and social competence is an automatic by-product of the school experience. Educators have painstakingly identified learner outcomes, selected curriculums and materials, and arranged learning interventions for every curricular area. Why have we left student discipline and social

Understanding Instructional Discipline

competencies unclear, undefined, and largely up to individual discretion? What are the social competencies we expect all students to have acquired upon graduation? School staff must work collaboratively to define desirable behaviors for school and life-long success and create learning routines to systematically teach and accelerate them.

▶ *Student discipline is best achieved through instruction rather than punishment.*

Some educators still believe that students would behave if we could just find a "bigger club," yet studies identify punishment as one of the least effective approaches (Lipsey, 1992). Historically schools have spent too much time trying to eliminate behaviors of concern rather than to accelerate desirable behaviors. Punishment focuses on what not to do and does not teach the child alternative successful ways to behave. Merely telling students that they are wrong and punishing them does not help them learn to do right. Effective schools realize that it is far easier and better to build adaptive behaviors through instructional approaches than to try to decrease maladaptive behaviors through punishment.

▶ *Student behavior can be taught using the same strategies used to teach academics.*

Behavior is learned, therefore, behavior can be taught. The strategies used to teach reading, math, science, etc., are the same strategies needed to teach social competency. Responsible behavior can be taught using direct instruction, practice, feedback, and encouragement. When social errors occur, our response should be correction–reteaching and arranging additional interventions and consequences as needed to ensure learning. In an instructional approach to discipline, misbehavior presents the student with an opportunity to learn and the educator with an opportunity to teach.

▶ *In order for behavior change to occur, we must use positive approaches that build relationships and a positive learning climate.*

While punishment temporarily suppresses inappropriate behavior, only positive approaches result in lasting behavior change. Effective schools avoid negative policies that emphasize "policing" or adversarial relationships and often result in mutual resentment and exclusionary practices. They realize that students are less likely to misbehave for teachers who they like and respect. Students today identify lack of respect as the number one problem facing our schools. Studies show that students will not engage in classes where there is little mutual respect, and if they do not engage, boredom and discipline problems ensue (Wagner, 1990). One secondary principal said it well, "In our school improvement efforts, changing the relationships between adults and students was at least as important as all the changes made in teaching, curriculum, and assessment."

▶ *Students need and want high standards for their behavior that are consistently upheld.*

A significant positive correlation exists between effective schools and high standards for appropriate behaviors. Unfortunately, educators often raise tolerances and lower their expectations for students who present frequent, chronic or challenging behaviors. Tolerating inappropriate behavior validates the behavior, and leads students to believe that teachers and administrators do not care about them. Studies show that students want teachers and administrators who: 1) are willing to take a stand for appropriate behavior, 2) are demanding in their expectations for academic work, and 3) are available to support and demonstrate care for students, providing the means for students to reach those expectations. Teachers with these characteristics have greater student respect and are less likely to be victimized by "tough" students (Boothe, et al. 1993).

Successful schools and teachers continually communicate high expectations for responsible behavior and actively teach, encourage, and hold students accountable for behaving in accordance with those expectations.

▶ *Services for students with chronic or intense behaviors are most effective within the context of a larger building-wide commitment to the social development of all students.*

Current trends in student discipline support a schoolwide approach. While individual student interventions remain necessary, they are not the most efficient response. An environment that proactively addresses *all* students' social and behavioral needs reduces the number and severity of problems and provides the conditions for greater success when more chronic or severe problems do occur. A collaborative schoolwide approach lays the groundwork for more effective individual interventions for students with chronic and intense behaviors.

▶ *There are few behavior problems that the school, family, and community working together cannot handle.*

This belief combines commitment and feelings of self-efficacy with collaborative problem solving structures. Effective schools see themselves as responsible for student success. Teachers have a personal sense of competence to produce positive changes in student behavior. Well-disciplined schools have a strong belief that good teaching can affect student performance regardless of background or presenting problems. They view their students as teachable and worthy of their attention and efforts.

Staff understand that for troubled and troublesome students their hope for learning responsible behavior rests with staying in school. Yet, none of us alone has all the answers. When challenging behavior occurs, effective schools use problem solving processes that are responsive to the student and staff's need for assistance, and seek to involve the family and community agencies as needed. When schools integrate comprehensive services for students we can adapt school conditions to successfully keep the child in his or her personal environment of home and school with those adults most committed to the child's long-term well being.

▶ *Schools, parents, and families should be partners in planning student success.*

The research on the value and role of parent involvement in education is clear–children's performance in school is improved when parents are involved. Parent involvement has demonstrated positive effects on achievement, attitude toward school, classroom behavior, time spent on homework, absenteesim, motivation, and expectations for one's future.

The earlier and more intensively parents are involved with their child's education, the greater the effects. Parent involvement also benefits the families through better school rapport that provides a system of support and leads to improved child-rearing practices and improved self-concepts (Cotton and Wikelund, 1989). Any school improvement effort must have parent involvement as a basic ingredient.

▶ *No matter how strong the discipline system, students will not develop positive behaviors if exposed to consistent failure experiences in the academic curriculum.*

Studies show that students experiencing discipline problems are failing on 7 out of 10 learning attempts. The concept of student discipline must be broad enough to include all the things teachers do to foster student involvement and cooperation in classroom activities and establish a productive work environment.

There is no doubt that if learning activities could be made more interesting, involving, and accessible to all, then problems of any kind, whether learning or behavioral difficulties, would be less likely to arise. A primary focus of discipline must thus be on the curriculum and the use of effective instructional methods.

Beliefs About Change and School Improvement

No matter how solid the understanding of best practices in discipline or the commitment to a common philosophy about student behavior, such a school improvement effort succeeds only if attention is paid to *how* change occurs and *what processes* are used to support the new learning and new practices. The beliefs that follow are derived from the change literature and the personal experiences of schools that were trailblazers in their work to make schools a more disciplined and successful place for all students.

▶ *More demanding school improvement efforts that are well implemented generate greater change and growth in teachers and lasting organizational improvement.*

If you attempt more, you will get more. Effective behavioral school improvement is perceived by staff as a significant, not an easy or trivial, effort that will affect the lives of students and staff on a daily basis. It is viewed as requiring significant changes in behavior and use of new practices by all staff. Successful schools realize that there is no "quick fix" for student discipline, but rather deep and thoughtful changes in attitudes and behavior that occur over time and significantly alter the learning climates (Purkey and Smith, 1983).

▶ *Strong leadership is the factor that contributes most directly and surely to ensuring that new practices are implemented and sustained.*

New practices entailing a significant amount of change, live or die by the vision, commitment, and amount of personal assistance received from the building leader. No single person has as much impact on the climate and discipline of the school as does the building administrator (Crandall & Loucks, 1983). Rutter, et al. (1979) states, "Schools with good outcomes had most decisions made at an administrative level with staff members' views clearly represented in the decisions." Strong leadership is an essential ingredient for behavioral school improvement.

▶ *Staff development makes the most difference in teacher behavior change and student achievement when the training is school-wide.*

The two most common mistakes in educational change are the underestimation of teacher training needs, and the absence of attention to the school culture and the structures necessary to support new procedures and staff behavior. Effective schools understand that change is a slow, difficult and gradual process for teachers. All staff must participate in training and development activities, and need to receive regular feedback on implementation efforts and continued support and follow-up after the initial training (Guskey, 1985).

▶ *Achieving consistency in staff behavior can only occur through collaborative planning and decision-making.*

Discipline is a *process,* not a *product.* It is a process of developing and gaining consensus on beliefs, expectations, and procedures, not just the completion of a written policy or staff discipline handbook. A well-written discipline plan developed and accepted only by a *few* and therefore poorly implemented accomplishes very little, while a plan that is developed, supported and fully implemented by *all* results in significant change. Only when staff act in unison in planning and development, will they act in unison in implementation. Full staff involvement in this process is crucial.

▶ *Sustained improvement will not occur without conscientious planning for the "institutionalization" of new practices.*

Implementation is a necessary, but not a sufficient, step toward lasting school improvement. Effective schools ensure that the project will become a part of their building long after the initial thrust or money is gone by writing it into policies, curricula and staff practices, eliminating competing practices, and incorporating it into supervision and evaluation practices (Crandall and Loucks, 1983).

▶ *Schools who view discipline as an ongoing process are more likely to experience lasting change.*

Discipline is not a one time or ad hoc committee responsibility. Effective schools realize that their discipline plan and procedures are continually evolving. They establish a standing leadership team and structure activities to ensure routine review and renewal through data gathering, training of new staff, policy revision, etc.

▶ *Schools that gather and use data to make decisions have a greater match between their needs and activities which lead to focused and meaningful staff development and greater satisfaction with outcomes.*

Too often, a school improvement project is launched with enthusiasm only to die a slow and quiet death. Data collection and analysis can keep discipline efforts alive by monitoring progress, promoting consistent implementation, identifying areas for renewal, and reinforcing and sustaining staff efforts through knowledge of results.

In summary, shared beliefs form the foundation for effective behavioral school improvement. A listing of these basic beliefs for an instructional approach to discipline can be found in Figure 3.

Beliefs for Instructional Discipline

- Education today must include a balanced focus on both academic achievement and social competency.
- Increasing behavioral concerns require building-wide, systematic and proactive approaches.
- Student discipline is best achieved through instruction rather than punishment.
- Student behavior can be taught using the same strategies used to teach academics.
- In order for behavior change to occur, we must use positive approaches that build relationships and a positive learning climate.
- Students need and want high standards for their behavior that are consistently upheld.
- Comprehensive services for students with chronic or intense problem behavior are most effective within the context of a larger building-wide commitment to the social and behavioral development of *all* students.
- There are few behavior problems that the school, family, and community working together cannot handle.
- Schools, parents, and families should be partners in planning student success.
- No matter how strong the discipline system, a student will not develop positive behaviors when exposed to consistent failure in the academic curriculum.

Figure 3

What Do We Want to Achieve?

Educators who approach discipline as a process of establishing and maintaining effective learning environments tend to be more successful than educators who place more emphasis on their roles as authority figures or disciplinarians.
— Good & Brophy (1994)

Meeting the discipline needs of today's schools at times appears an overwhelming task complicated by emotions and confusing or seemingly conflicting recommendations from the experts. For the building administrator, managing fair and effective discipline procedures must, at times, be frightening. For teachers, being asked to shift the emphasis of instruction from a solely academic curriculum to a combination of academics and social behaviors, the question might be, "How much more can we do?"

There is, however, a new and growing body of research and experience available on instructionally-based approaches that promise improved outcomes, not only for students with discipline problems, but for all students. These schoolwide practices and individual student supports provide educators with sound principles and practical strategies that not only affect discipline, but also school climate, relationships with students, and learning.

Schoolwide Discipline

While perhaps phrased differently, discipline experts identify similar features that are essential to effective schoolwide discipline: 1) clear expectations, 2) strategies to teach those expectations to all students, 3) the high visibility of all staff, supervising and watching for expected behaviors, 4) strategies to provide frequent feedback–both positive and corrective, and 5) positive relationships between adults and students. All five pieces of the puzzle must be in place for responsible behavior to flourish; if any one of these schoolwide elements is weak or absent, outcomes are diminished. Each is discussed below.

1. Clear Expectations

Just as schools realize academic success because of the direction provided by their academic curriculums, success with student discipline begins with clear student behavioral expectations. This *behavioral curriculum* is not a list of prohibitive rules, but a vision of responsible student behavior and social competence.

A behavioral curriculum limits inconsistent reactions by staff to student misbehaviors. Agreed upon student expectations promote consistency across staff through a common language and assist staff to develop similar tolerance levels. A behavioral curriculum allows educators to be proactive, focusing on catching students behaving responsibly. Only then can staff work in unison to systematically teach and encourage responsible behavior, rather than merely attempt to suppress misbehavior. The curriculum provides the standards to teach and measure social outcomes.

A comprehensive behavioral curriculum begins with general guiding principles, and then further clarifies those principles through a social skills curriculum and specific common area expectations and classroom procedures or routines.

Guiding principles. Principles that define attitudes and behaviors for long-term success and behavioral growth are the foundation of a behavioral curriculum. Often called "Guidelines for Success," these principles emphasize a higher level of moral reasoning rather than merely focusing on rules and consequences (Sprick & Garrison, 1992). They are statements of valued behaviors and attitudes such as respect, responsibility, cooperation, learning and effort. They communicate high expectations and show students how they can be successful, not only in school but also in life. These guiding principles govern how we treat each other in all school settings, and replace longer lists of rules.

Social skills. Many schools identify interpersonal competencies that embody their guiding principles and offer a set of life-long skills for success (Kain, Downs & Black, 1988). A social skills curriculum assists educators to go beyond merely lamenting about student misbehavior, allowing them to teach responsible behaviors. Social skills provide staff with the specific content for their formal and informal daily interactions with students, and provide students with a clearer understanding of what is "successful" behavior.

Common area expectations. Schools further help students to be successful by clarifying expectations for behavior in common areas of their building. Common areas typically include hallways, cafeteria, recess or breaks, arrival/departure times, assemblies, and sporting events, etc. A clear understanding of responsibility in these areas increases staff comfort and consistency during supervision and increases the likelihood of accountable student behavior (Colvin & Lazar, 1997; Sprick & Garrison, 1992).

Classroom procedures. While classroom procedures may vary from teacher to teacher, we do not find effectively run classrooms without them (Evertson & Emmer, 1996). Clear classroom procedures minimize the amount of non-academic time students spend in school, increase instructional time, ensure a positive learning climate, and provide students with productive work habits that lead to personal accountability and effectiveness now and in the future. In effective schools, *every* staff contributes to the well-disciplined atmosphere by defining successful student behaviors for teacher-led instruction, participation, independent work, movement in and out of their room, small group work, and other procedures such as homework and grading.

In addition to guiding principles, a social skills curriculum, common area expectations, and classroom procedures, schools may also further clarify successful behaviors through conflict management, self-advocacy, peer mediation or anger control curriculums.

A behavioral curriculum, consistently upheld, is one of the most important aspects of effective discipline.

2. <u>Preventive Teaching</u>

Once behavioral expectations have been defined, student acquisition of desirable behaviors is most effectively managed through systematic teaching. This teaching calls upon the same methods used to teach academic skills—direct instruction, practice, and feedback.

At the beginning of school and as necessary throughout the year, students should be taught the guidelines for success, social skills, and how to behave responsibly in each school setting. Research shows that effective teachers spend approximately one-third of their time during the first days or weeks of the new school year teaching their expectations (Evertson & Emmer, 1993). This preventive teaching includes three basic strategies:

Group lessons. Introduction of guiding principles, social skills or procedures to an entire class or building is typically done through group lessons. When helping students learn responsible behavior, the old adage, *"teaching is not telling, and learning is not having been told,"* is certainly true. Effective behavioral instruction incorporates all the elements of lesson design and goes beyond "telling" to include modeling, checking for understanding, and opportunities for guided and unguided practice and feedback (Paine, 1983).

The amount of time spent on behavioral instruction will vary depending on the age and sophistication of students, whether behavior has been particularly problematic in the past, the presence of a highly mobile population, or if students come from homes with conflicting ways of behaving.

Individual instruction. Additional teaching or review of expectations with individual students or small groups is often necessary. Effective teachers use brief personal learning opportunities as needed for those students who have difficulties or require more frequent teaching in order to be successful. A quick review of expectations with students who need this ongoing assistance (e.g., students with ADHD or other learning or behavioral difficulties) embodies the understanding that "an ounce of prevention is worth a pound of cure," and sets them up for success.

Preventive prompts. Brief reminders of an expectation or skill provided just before an opportunity to use that expectation, skill or procedure, help to encourage responsible student behavior and diminish the need for correction. Effective teachers use preventive prompts to elicit desirable student behavior at a high frequency.

Teaching of the behavioral curriculum should also include a plan to ensure that new students are provided the opportunity to learn the behaviors that will lead to success in their new school.

3. High Staff Visibility & Supervision

Madeline Hunter is remembered to say, "You must *INspect* what you *EXpect.*" Her assertion reflects an often-overlooked yet critical element of schoolwide discipline–*supervision.* No matter how thoroughly student expectations are defined and taught, if staff are not visible in all areas of the building, interacting with students and watching for responsible behaviors, students are not likely to consistently behave in accordance with these expectations.

Well-disciplined schools thoughtfully attend to the supervision of students, using this time to interact positively, provide a model of appropriate behavior, clarify tolerance levels, and build relationships with students. An effective schoolwide discipline plan addresses staff expectations for high visibility and supervision of students in all common areas and activities.

4. Frequent Feedback

Staff must not only teach, model, and watch for appropriate behavior, but must also provide feedback to students about their behavioral progress. This feedback or *incidental teaching* capitalizes on naturally occurring opportunities to reinforce students who demonstrate responsible behavior or provide correction to students who behave irresponsibly. It is this feedback, consistently provided by staff, which sustains student effort and results in lasting behavior change. Feedback strategies include both positive feedback and corrective teaching.

Positive feedback. The most important means of encouraging students to behave responsibly are the minute-by-minute interactions that occur between staff and students. Creating a school culture where responsible behavior is the norm requires that staff interact with students four times more frequently when they have engaged in responsible behavior than when the student is misbehaving. This ratio of 4:1 positive to negative interactions may simply include compliments and general praise, or may include more specific descriptive feedback known as *effective praise* (Black et al, 1987).

Corrective teaching. Misbehavior must be viewed as a teaching opportunity—a chance to clarify and reteach expectations. The same calm instructional approach used when students make academic errors should be used to correct social errors. *Corrective teaching* interrupts the behavior needing improvement so that a more appropriate response can be taught, practiced and then reinforced. With this approach, educators manage student misbehavior through instruction (Downs, Kutsick & Black, 1985).

Associated with feedback is the use of consequences. In an instructional approach to discipline, consequences are not so much to reward or punish, but to enhance or extend teaching, providing students with the motivation and practice opportunities necessary for them to begin behaving in acceptable ways.

When dealing with misbehavior, staff must understand that it is not the *severity* of the consequence but the *inevitability* or certainty that a response will occur which affects student behavior. It is less important *what* the negative consequence is, than that *something* is consistently done. Many teachers report uncertainty about consequences as the reason they do not address student misbehavior. Therefore, it is essential that staff have a full menu of mild logical consequences (+ and –) that are easy to use, increasing their certainty of responding.

Effective negative consequences are those that are relevant to the behavior, individually selected to match learner needs, and mildly aversive yet educational—that is, they help the student to learn and demonstrate the desirable behavior. Consequences should be considerate of student dignity and, when appropriate, encourage students to make amends to those offended.

Establishing a sense of responsibility and self-discipline in students is an *ongoing* teaching process, not a one time teaching task. Frequent feedback and an instructional use of consequences are hallmarks of a well-disciplined school.

5. <u>Positive Relationships</u>

Being technically sound in the use of expectations, teaching, supervision, feedback and consequences is essential to schoolwide discipline, but for those factors to be effective, they must be combined with strong relationships. The quality of teacher-student relationships has great influence on the amount of productive or disruptive behavior students display in school (Jones & Jones, 1995).

However, neither the old adage, "never smile until Christmas," nor the belief that *all* classroom problems can be solved with love and understanding are very helpful in creating a climate where responsible behavior flourishes. Students want teachers who maintain high standards for behavior and learning yet demonstrate care, concern and the availability to help them achieve those standards. Only when high expectations are combined with relationship-building behaviors such as positive feedback, respect for privacy, communicating in close proximity, listening, eye contact, pleasant voice tone, smiles, touch, and use of students' names will their attitudes about school and its staff be positive.

Individual Student Supports

When implementing proactive and positive approaches to discipline, we know that the majority of students will strive to meet our expectations. However, we also know that no single set of procedures will work to help every student be responsible. Schools must design interventions for students who display more chronic or intense behaviors (Tobin, Sugai, & Colvin, 1996). Figure 4 depicts this continuum of behavioral needs and the support necessary for all students to find success in school.

The focus of our work with disruptive students remains positive and instructional. We realize that we live in a culture where an education is critical to success. Therefore, we must strive to keep even the most troubled and challenging students in school and teach them to be successful. We also realize that no individual is expected to have all the answers. Working with challenging students requires a team approach. The following six beliefs guide our responses to these students:

- Teachers must first assess their classroom climate and management methods to determine if they are consistent with best practice.

- Staff have a responsibility to use methods aimed at teaching and altering students' behavior, not punishment.

- Teachers need to receive immediate assistance from administrators or others designated to help when students persist in disrupting the classroom learning.

- Support for ongoing problems must include opportunities for collaboration and problem solving with a team of "experts" who can develop an individual behavioral plan.

- Outside consultation should be provided when a student continues behavioral difficulties despite the above efforts.

- Schools can best serve students with intense problems when procedures are in place for coordinating efforts with the family and other community resources or agencies.

A brief description of best practices in providing individual student supports follows.

1. <u>Support for Classroom Disruptions</u>

Discipline is a shared responsibility between administration and staff, and must not fall solely into the lap of either one or the other. The teacher is accountable for ensuring that students clearly understand the behavioral expectations and for using effective strategies to promote

What Do We Want to Achieve?

high levels of responsible student behavior. It is the administrator's responsibility to support their teachers in working with students whose chronic misbehaviors disrupt the learning environment.

Students need to know that they will not be allowed to disrupt their learning or the learning of others. When disruptive behavior occurs, it is unrealistic to expect teachers to spend long periods of time working with an uncooperative student, if for no other reason than it erodes instructional time and diminishes the belief that class time is valued and to be used wisely. To uphold this value for learning, staff must work collaboratively and clarify *when* to refer students to the office.

Disruptions often evoke responses in adults that limit their patience and creativity and turn into a desire to have the student removed so that someone else can assume responsibility. While support must be available for disruptive students, if removal from class is used too soon or too frequently, the impact is diminished, it runs counter to student needs, and may even violate student rights. Staff, working together, need to define when a student is "out of instructional control." This definition provides the framework for staff to make effective decisions.

Time spent with the administrator during a discipline referral can be a valuable learning opportunity for students with the greatest need, and it helps teachers to maintain a precedence for safe and responsible behavior in their classrooms. Thoughtful planning for this support is essential.

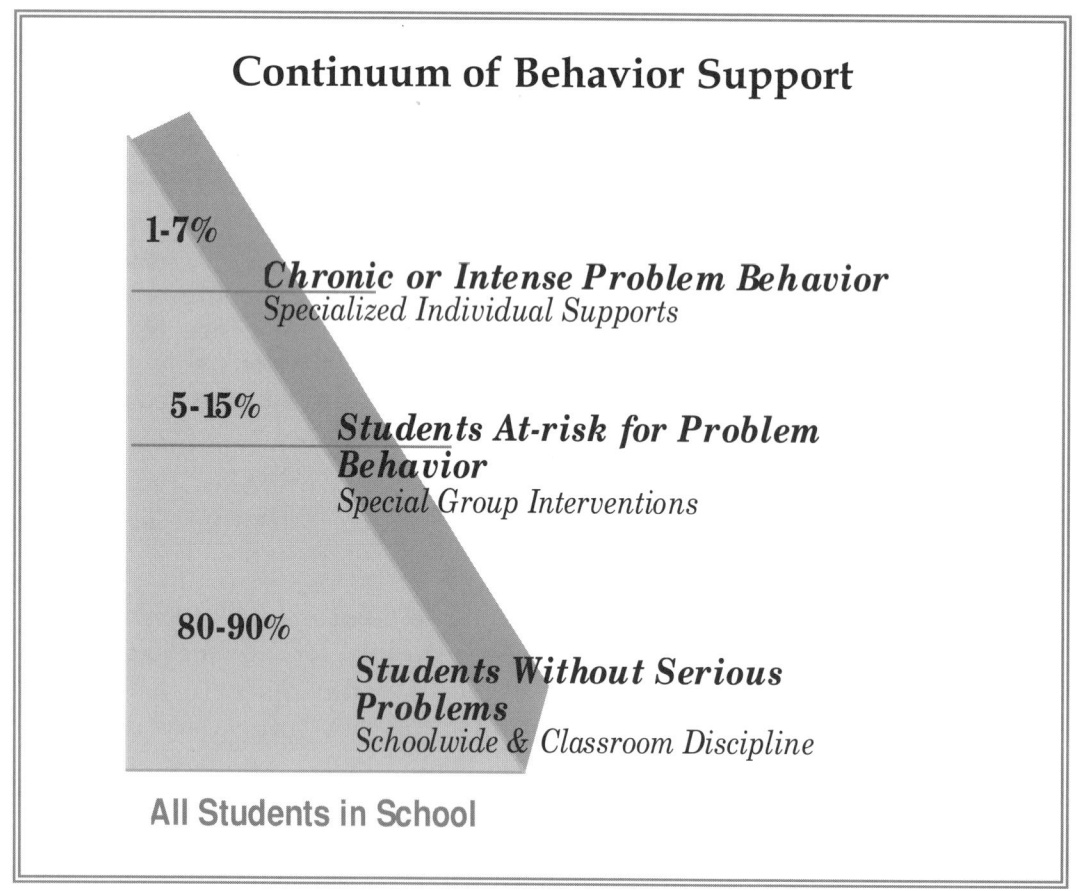

Figure 4

2. <u>Team-based Planning & Problem Solving</u>

Despite their best intentions, teachers can become frustrated by the persistent irresponsible behavior of a student or a group and may find it difficult to analyze the situation and develop effective behavior change strategies. A problem solving team offers staff the security and comfort of timely assistance and the stimulation needed to maintain their focus and energy when working with difficult students (Sugai, 1998).

Behavior Support Teams are comprised of teachers, administrators, and support staff that possess the knowledge of specialized behavioral interventions necessary to address complex student problems. The team works collaboratively with the teacher to analyze the problem and design strategies to assist the student in improving his or her behavior (Sugai, G. 1998). These teams can request additional assistance through the more formal problem solving process (SAT, BAT, etc.) that offers additional resources and the involvement of other service providers as needed. Effective schools ensure that the competencies to work with challenging students are developed within the ranks of the building staff.

3. <u>Individual Behavior Plans</u>

The team-based problem solving process should result in the development of an *individual behavior plan*. Based on a functional assessment of the student's behavior, this comprehensive plan details strategies and interventions that have been personally matched to student needs. Individual behavior plans clearly identify strategies and staff responsibilities for their implementation, while providing the means to monitor student progress and make adjustments as needed. A well-developed individual behavior plan leads to greater accountability and increased student success.

4. <u>School, Home, and Community Collaboration</u>

With an instructional approach to discipline, staff are charged with using a wide range of preventive and corrective approaches for students. However, the educational focus of our responsibilities and staff preparation sometimes limit our ability to respond to the most serious needs of some students. It is therefore important that schools establish collaborative relationships and procedures to readily access community agencies charged with meeting the more complex needs that are beyond the scope of the school.

District and building procedures should be created to facilitate networking among school staff, parents, social service agencies, law enforcement, the juvenile justice system, and other relevant community resources. Joint planning ensures the most effective and comprehensive services while preventing duplication of effort or even incompatible efforts, and keeping everyone informed, ensuring greater success.

While a planful arrangement with other child-serving agencies may be a critical part of ensuring an education for students with chronic or intense behaviors, working with community agencies should not lead to an abdication of responsibility by the school for developing needed services for troubled and troublesome students.

To successfully address student discipline, schools must thoughtfully address both schoolwide practices and individual student supports.

What Do We Want to Achieve?

Instructional Discipline

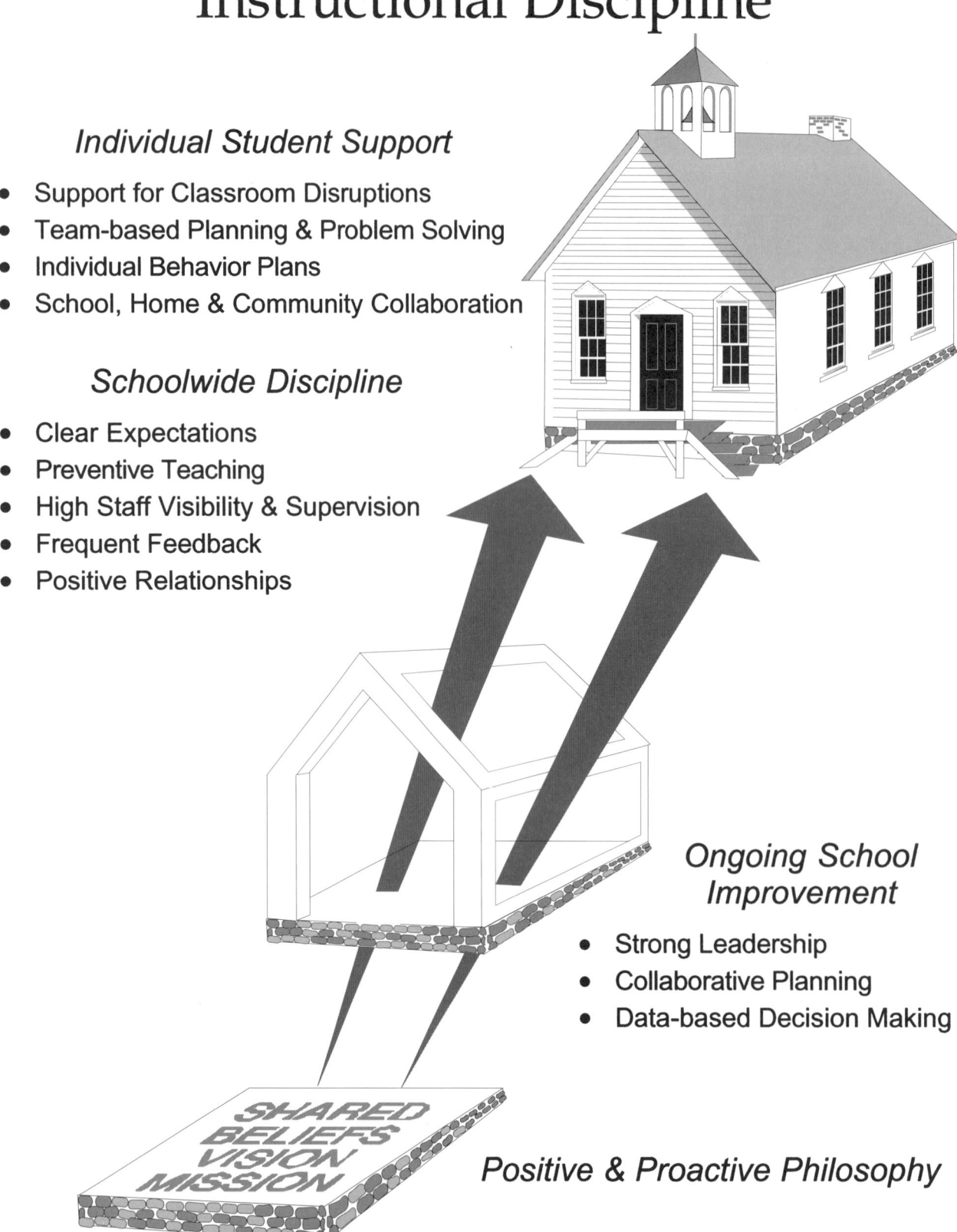

Individual Student Support

- Support for Classroom Disruptions
- Team-based Planning & Problem Solving
- Individual Behavior Plans
- School, Home & Community Collaboration

Schoolwide Discipline

- Clear Expectations
- Preventive Teaching
- High Staff Visibility & Supervision
- Frequent Feedback
- Positive Relationships

Ongoing School Improvement

- Strong Leadership
- Collaborative Planning
- Data-based Decision Making

Positive & Proactive Philosophy

Figure 5

Solving the Discipline Puzzle

Achieving the Vision

In schools with good discipline, the staffs believe in their school and in what its students can do, and they expend unusual amounts of energy to make that belief come true.

— Phi Delta Kappa
Commission on Discipline, 1982

When initiating behavioral school improvement, understanding the elements of schoolwide discipline and individual student support is not enough. Schools must also use methods that blend these proven practices with effective school improvement processes, thereby promoting deep and lasting change.

Positive and Proactive Philosophy

One of the first steps is to examine staff beliefs about behavior and their role in discipline. *Having* beliefs to guide the effort is much less important than the *process* of discovering them, the process by which they become shared. Beliefs imposed on staff, at best, command compliance. Discovering shared beliefs increases commitment and often is the first step in unifying staff, allowing people who may mistrust each other to begin to work together.

Effective schools commit their philosophy of discipline to writing through their beliefs, vision and mission. This philosophy creates the sense of direction that gives coherence to diverse activities and keeps the learning on course when stresses develop. Without a common philosophy to pull staff toward the goal, to compel new ways of thinking and acting, the forces in support of the status quo can be overwhelming. Time spent examining what staff truly believe about student discipline and creating a shared philosophy is a wise investment in lasting change.

Ongoing School Improvement

1. <u>Strong Leadership</u>

Successful school improvement efforts all share one commonality —strong leadership. Maintaining a well-disciplined school is one of the primary roles of the building administrator. Therefore, the personal commitment of a principal or other administrator to school climate and student discipline is essential.

In addition, the continual process of developing and maintaining student discipline requires the formation of a leadership team. The *discipline leadership team* is a standing committee responsible for developing and maintaining effective procedures and a positive school environment. Formed to provide leadership, this team is not to assume sole responsibility for developing a schoolwide discipline plan. Instead, they thoughtfully involve the entire staff in rethinking their beliefs about student behavior, reviewing existing procedures, and developing and maintaining effective practices.

Effective teams are comprised of 5-7 members with full representation of building staff. Collective membership leads to a greater assurance that all staff members' views will be represented and that the team's leadership will be widely accepted by all teachers, paraprofessionals, specialists, and administrators.

The team should include staff members who are "doers," held in high esteem by their colleagues, and team players who focus on solutions and are positive and persuasive in their interactions with staff, students, and parents. Team members are responsible for planning and leading the many activities related to this school improvement effort such as presenting data, facilitating planning and decision-making meetings, arranging for or providing skill training, and modeling, guiding, and encouraging others.

Since schoolwide discipline is an ongoing process, not merely the completion of a product or document, the leadership team is an ongoing committee. Participation on the team over time should be shared and, therefore, the membership rotated. Careful planning of the team's role, composition, responsibilities, and length of term are important variables to consider before beginning.

2. Collaborative Planning

Schoolwide discipline planning should not be viewed as either a top-down or a bottom-up procedure. Rather it is a collaborative venture with administration, the leadership team and staff all working together.

Ad hoc work groups or committees do much of the practice and procedure development, with all staff participating on a work group of their choice. The work they do will be brought in draft form before the entire staff for discussion, revision, and finally determining consensus.

When everyone has a hand in developing discipline procedures, ownership is increased, consensus is more readily obtained, and consistent implementation of procedures more likely. The more difficulty that is anticipated (e.g., the amount of change required, a current lack of cohesiveness among staff, weak communication between grade levels or between administration and staff, etc.), the more important it is to use collaborative processes that involve the entire staff.

Again, discipline is a *process,* not a *product*—a process of developing and gaining consensus on beliefs, expectations and procedures, not just the completion of a written policy or staff handbook. Full staff involvement in this process is crucial.

3. Data-based Decision-making

Use of data can focus staff's efforts by identifying areas in need of improvement, and keep the effort alive by providing feedback or knowledge of results that promote consistent implementation and renewal.

There are several methods useful for gathering and evaluating school discipline procedures:

Surveys–A questionnaire or interview which asks individuals (staff, administrators, students, and parents) to share their beliefs, perceptions or experiences related to school discipline. Change in perception is particularly useful as discipline procedures significantly impact the building climate or how we think and feel about school.

Observations–Periodic planned visits to classrooms or common areas for observing and recording the kinds of behaviors displayed by students, the interactions that occur among teachers and students, and the level and effectiveness of supervision. Observations can confirm or clarify the perception data gathered through surveys.

Behavioral Records–Using available

and easily retrieved data from existing school records (e.g., office referrals, attendance, tardies, detentions, suspensions, referrals to the BAT or SAT, referrals to special education, etc.) This objective data is particularly meaningful.

Behavior Rating Scales–Staff evaluate students' use of specific social skills and behaviors in specific situations.

Data collection is not a one-time project, but rather an ongoing process that allows staff to assess the kinds and amounts of changes being prompted by the application of the discipline procedures. As staff gather and analyze data, they find areas where implementation is weak or inconsistent, or where policies need upgrading or extending. This data can identify the need for increased supervision, staff development, revision of practices or new procedure development.

Another major purpose for gathering and analyzing student behavioral data is identifying any trends that may indicate the presence of disparity in treatment of students by race, gender, age, or ethnicity. The review of data assures that objective, fair and equitable responses to misbehaving students are being made.

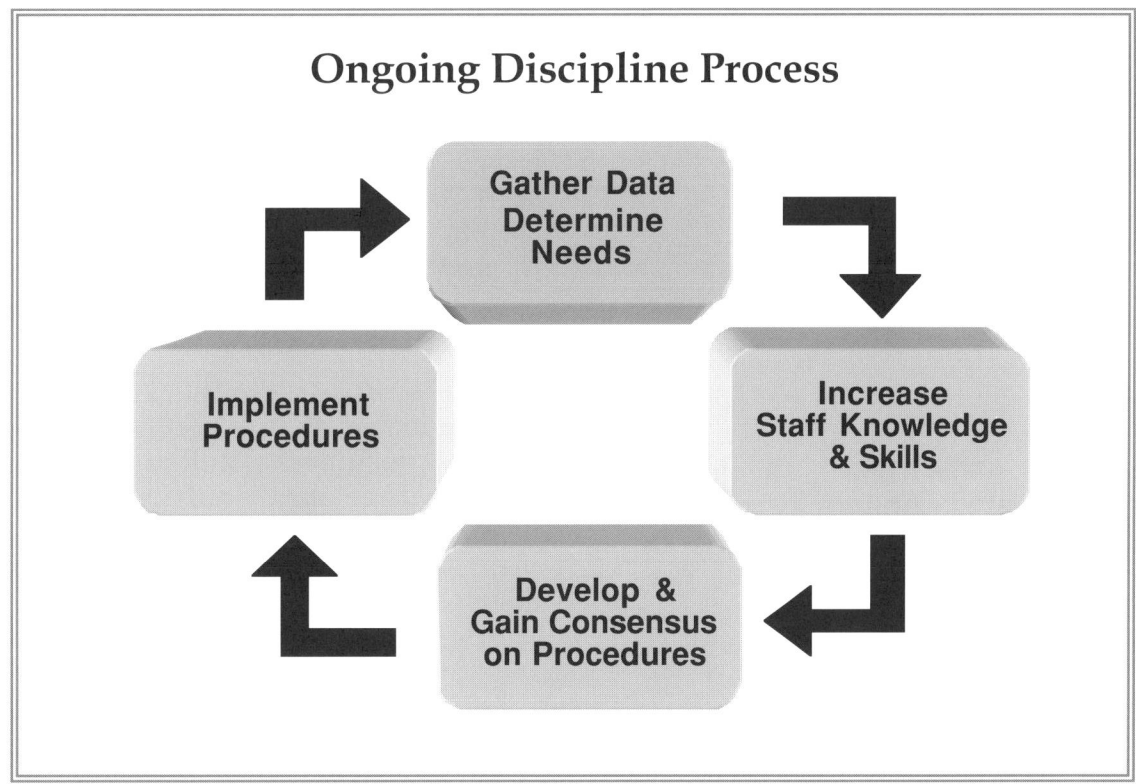

Figure 6

The ongoing improvement process begins by gathering data to determine what is working and what is not—to establish needs and prioritize areas for improvement or development. Staff training to help staff acquire the knowledge and skills necessary to proceed is then followed by full staff involvement in the development of practices and procedures. When consensus is reached on these practices, plans for implementation are made. The cycle continues with the gathering of data to provide feedback on the new practices, offering the vehicle for procedure or practice revision and renewal, and for ensuring equity in the use of discipline procedures.

In summary, the process of building a school culture of respect and responsibility begins with a solid foundation of shared beliefs, a vision, and mission that are founded in a *Positive and Proactive Philosophy*. Next, a framework of *Ongoing School Improvement* processes is essential to support the development of *Schoolwide Discipline* practices and *Individual Student Supports*. These components are illustrated in figure 5 on page 26.

Determining Readiness

Careful consideration of readiness to undertake behavioral school improvement is wise and can be done by confirming the presence of conditions known to predict success. These conditions include:

- *Perceived Need.* Staff should be in agreement that change in schoolwide discipline is warranted. This need should be documented through perception, observation, and/or record review data, and as a result, student social development or schoolwide discipline should be one of the top three school improvement goals.

- *Leadership.* The building administrator(s) must be aware of his/her role relative to student social development and schoolwide discipline, and be willing to remain actively involved in all training and development activities as well as oversee staff implementation and accountability. The creation of a *discipline leadership team* to facilitate development, implementation and ongoing maintenance of discipline procedures is also critical.

- *Collaborative processes.* The administrator and staff must be committed to a schoolwide process involving *all* staff. The presence of team-based structures (e.g. study groups, support teams or grade level teams) and regularly scheduled staff meeting times are necessary for planning and consensus building. Decision-making procedures must be clear.

- *Shared beliefs, mission and philosophy.* The school staff must share a common mission of both academic and social success for all students, and a positive, proactive and instructional philosophy of student discipline.

- *Commitment.* Administration and staff must be willing to commit to active and long-term participation in staff development, and the ongoing monitoring of schoolwide discipline practices.

- *Accountability.* Administration and staff must be willing to produce the written documents and to continuously gather and analyze data as necessary to ensure staff commitment to and maintenance of newly developed practices and procedures.

The School Profile

The *School Profile* beginning on page 31 provides a review of all elements of Instructional Discipline. It also serves as a self-assessment, allowing schools to determine where they stand compared to the vision. Used by teams or individuals for reflection, it can stimulate small group discussion, help staff consider strengths and weaknesses, leading to a commitment to engage in a school improvement effort.

School ✓ Profile

Instructional Discipline: Where Do We Stand?

✓ Positive and Proactive Philosophy

☐ 1. In our school, we have a philosophy of discipline (vision, beliefs and mission) that reflects positive and proactive approaches, and is in writing and included in our discipline policy or school handbook.

☐ 2. In our school, we continually communicate our positive and proactive philosophy to others (parents, community, new staff, etc.), and it is used to make related school decisions.

☐ 3. In our school, staff behavior is congruent with this positive and proactive approach to discipline.

✓ Ongoing School Improvement

☐ 4. In our school, we have a standing committee or leadership team responsible for guiding our discipline efforts.

☐ 5. In our school, the process for development or review of discipline procedures involves all staff, uses consensus to reach decision, and keeps everyone well informed.

☐ 6. In our school, sufficient training has occurred to ensure staff have the knowledge and skills needed to implement our schoolwide discipline practices.

☐ 7. In our school, we support each other and sustain staff efforts through frequent opportunities for sharing, consultation, peer coaching, and feedback on results, etc. Staff are regularly recognized for their contributions to a well-disciplined school.

☐ 8. In our school, outcomes are monitored through data collection (office referral patterns, common area observations, surveys, etc.) and results are regularly shared with staff.

☐ 9. In our school, assistance is provided to staff needing help in implementing instructional discipline approaches. Plans are made to work with resistant staff.

✓ Schoolwide Discipline

• *Clear Expectations*

☐ 10. In our school, we have guiding principles (Guidelines for Success) that define our vision of the "successful students."

☐ 11. In our school, we have a social skills curriculum that more specifically clarifies those guiding principles.

☐ 12. In our school, we have clearly defined student expectations for each of our building's common areas (hallways, cafeteria, recess/breaks, etc.).

☐ 13. In our school, each teacher has clarified procedures for success in their classroom.

☐ 14. In our school, we have plans (bulletin boards, newsletters, open house, etc.) to continually share and review our behavioral expectations with students and parents.

☐ 15. In our school, we have identified other curricula (conflict resolution, problem solving, anger control, etc.) necessary to help all students achieve social competence.

• *Preventive Teaching*

☐ 16. In our school, we have an annual plan for teaching and practicing our behavioral curriculum (guidelines for success, common area expectations, social skills, classroom procedures) with all students.

☐ 17. In our school, we have special activities or events (assemblies, contests, skill of the week, etc.) to ensure building-wide involvement in teaching responsible behavior.

☐ 18. In our school, all staff (including specialists and support staff) participate in teaching our behavioral curriculum to students.

☐ 19. In our school, staff regularly use individual teaching and preventive prompts to review and practice expectations and social skills with students who need additional assistance.

☐ 20. In our school, we have orientation procedures for introducing our behavioral expectations to new students.

✓ Schoolwide Discipline–*Continued*

• *High Staff Visibility and Supervision*

☐ 21. In our school, we have determined the supervision needs for each of our building's common areas and have specific staff supervision assignments to ensure high staff visibility.

☐ 22. In our school, staff responsibilities during supervision are clearly described in writing for each common area.

☐ 23. In our school, staff maintain low tolerances and consistently uphold the common area expectations with students.

☐ 24. In our school, staff are highly visible and positively interact with students throughout our building.

• *Frequent Feedback (+ and -)*

☐ 25. In our school, staff use positive feedback at a high rate (4:1) to inform students of their behavioral progress.

☐ 26. In our school, we have a building-wide incentive system to encourage students to use responsible behaviors and we use it enthusiastically and consistently.

☐ 27. In our school, we have a menu of mild positive consequences to use selectively when encouraging individual student behavior.

☐ 28. In our school, staff view social errors as opportunities to teach our behavioral expectations. When problem behaviors occur, staff calmly correct through re-teaching.

☐ 29. In our school, staff maintain low tolerances and consistently correct students whose behaviors deviates from the expectations.

☐ 30. In our school, we have a menu of mild logical negative consequences to use in conjunction with our corrective teaching.

☐ 31. In our school, consequences are individually selected to match student learning needs (not predetermined, used rigidly or unilaterally).

☐ 32. In our school, feedback is done respectfully.

✓ Schoolwide Discipline–*Continued*

• *Positive Relationships*

☐ 33. In our school, staff model the same responsible behaviors and positive attitudes expected of students.

☐ 34. In our school, staff maintain high rates of positive interactions with students, their peers, and parents.

☐ 35. In our school, staff and students smile and greet each other.

☐ 36. In our school, staff regularly use relationship-building behaviors (smile, name, touch, eye contact, etc.) to convey interest and caring when interacting with students.

☐ 37. In our school, staff support each other and work collaboratively toward developing responsible student behavior.

✓ Individual Student Supports

• *Support for Classroom Disruptions*

☐ 38. In our school, staff use preferred behaviors that de-escalate and diffuse students who are angry, defensive, or non-compliant.

☐ 39. In our school, we have defined "out of instructional control" and staff clearly understand when to refer students to the office.

☐ 40. In our school, when students have a discipline referral the administrator and staff communicate with one another before and after to ensure successful interventions.

☐ 41. In our school, we have interventions for more serious or chronic behaviors that assist students to use responsible behavior, encourage restitution, and eliminate "push out practices." (detentions, suspensions, Saturday school, etc.)

• *Team-based Planning and Problem Solving*

☐ 42. In our school, procedures are in place for swift collaboration and problem solving on students with chronic or severe problems. (e.g., Teacher Assistance Team)

☐ 43. In our school, the problem solving team has expertise in interventions for challenging students and assist in the development and monitoring of an individual behavior plan.

✓ Individual Student Supports–*Continued*

- *School, Home and Community Collaboration*

☐ 44. In our school, we planfully share discipline information with all parents (e.g., handbooks, newsletters, open houses, etc.)

☐ 45. In our school, parents know, understand and are supportive of our discipline procedures.

☐ 46. In our school, parents' opinions are valued; parents are routinely involved in planning for their child's discipline.

☐ 47. In our school, we have procedures that allow for the efficient and meaningful engagement of other child-serving agencies when planning for students with more intense behavior difficulties.

☐ 48. In our school, we have procedures to respond to crisis or other dangerous situations.

NOTES

References

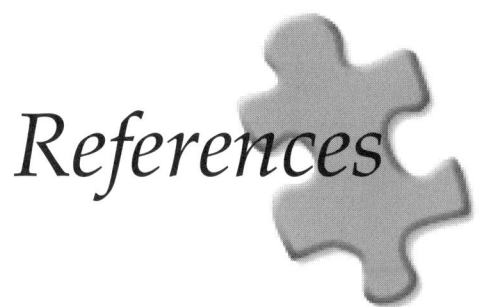

Baer, D.M., Wolf, M.M., & Risley, T.R. (1968). Some Current Dimensions of Applied Behavior Analysis. *Journal of Applied Behavior Analysis*, Vol. 1, pp. 91-97.

Boothe, et al. (1993). The Violence at Your Door. Executive Educator.

Black, D.D., Downs, J.C. Brown, L. & Wells, P.L. (1987). *Motivation Systems, Social Skills in the Schools,* and *Administrative Intervention.* Boys Town, NE: Father Flanagan's Boy's Home.

Borich, G.D. (1977). *The Appraisal of Teaching: Concepts and Process.* Reading, MA: Addison Wesley.

Broussard, C.D., & Northup, J. (1995). An Approach to Functional Assessment and Analysis of Disruptive Behavior in Regular Education Classrooms. *School Psychology Quarterly*, Vol. 10, pp.151-164.

Center for Effective Collaboration and Practice (1998). *Addressing Student Problem Behavior: An IEP Team's Introduction to Functional Behavioral Assessment and Behavior Intervention Plans.* Washington, DC: American Institute for Research.

Colvin, G. (1997). *Managing Acting-Out Behavior.* Longmont, CO: Sopris West, Inc.

Colvin, G., Kame'enui, E.J., & Sugai, G. (1993). Schoolwide and Classroom Management: Reconceptualizing the Integration and Management of Students with Behavior Problems in General Education. *Education and Treatment of Children*, Vol. 16, pp. 361-381.

Colvin, G., & Lazar, M. (1997). *The Effective Elementary Classroom: Managing for Success.* Longmont, CO: Sopris West, Inc.

Colvin, G., & Sprick, R. (1999). Providing Administrative Leadership for Effective Behavior Support: Ten Strategies for Principals. *Effective School Practices*, Vol. 17, pp. 65-71.

Colvin, G., & Sugai, G. (1988). Proactive Strategies for Managing Social Behavior Problems: An Instructional Approach. *Education and Treatment of Children.* Vol. 12, No. 4, pp.341-348.

Colvin, G., Sugai, G., Good, R.H., & Lee, Y. (1997). Using Active Supervision and Precorrection to Improve Transition Behaviors in an Elementary School. *School Psychology Quarterly,* Vol. 12, pp. 344-363.

Cotton, K. (1990). Schoolwide and Classroom Discipline. *School Improvement Research Series.* Portland, OR: Northwest Regional Educational Laboratory.

Cotton, K., & Wikelund (1989). Parent Involvement in Education. *School Improvement Research Series.* Portland, OR: Northwest Regional Educational Laboratory.

Covaleskie, J. (1992). Discipline and Morality: Beyond Rules and Consequences. *Education Forum.*

Crandall, D., and Loucks, S. (1983). *People, Policies, and Practices: Examining the Chain of School Improvement, Vol. I-X.* Andover, MA: The Network, Inc.

Crews, G.A. (1997). *The Evolution of School Disturbance in America.* Westport, CT: Praeger.

Curwin, R. L. and Mendler, A. N. (1988). *Discipline With Dignity.* Alexandria, VA: Association for Supervision and Curriculum Development.

Downs, J., Kutsick, J. and Black D. (1985). The Teaching Interaction: A Systematic Approach to Developing Social Skills in Disruptive and Non-Disruptive Students. *Techniques: A Journal for Remedial Education and Counseling,* Vol. 1.

Dunlap, G., Kern-Dunlap, L., Clarke, S., & Robbins, F.R. (1991). Functional Assessment, Curricular Revision, and Severe Behavior Problems. *Journal of Applied Behavior Analysis,* Vol. 24, pp. 387-397.

References

Evertson, C. & Emmer, E. (1996). *Classroom Management for Elementary Teachers; Classroom Management for Secondary Teachers*, Fourth Edition. Needham Heights, MA: Allyn and Bacon.

Foster-Johnson, L., & Dunlap, G. (1993). Using Functional Assessment to Develop Effective, Individualized Interventions for Challenging Behaviors. *Teaching Exceptional Children,* Vol. 25, pp. 44-50.

Gathercoal, F. (1993). *Judicious Discipline.* Third Edition. San Francisco, CO: Caddo Gap Press.

Good, T.L. and Brophy, J.E. (1994). *Looking in Classrooms.* Fifth Edition. New York, NY: Harper & Row.

Gossen, D. (1993). *Restitution: Restructuring School Discipline*. New View Publications. Chapel Hill, NC.

Gresham, F.M. (1981). Assessment of Children's Social Skills. *Journal of School Psychology,* Vol. 19, No 2, pp. 120-33.

Guskey, T. (1985). Staff Development and the Process of Teacher Change. *Educational Researcher.* Vol. 15, No. 5, pp. 5-12.

Harvard Education Letter. (1988). Entire issue, Vol. 3, No. 5.

Horner, R.H., (1994). Functional Assessment: Contributions and Future Directions. *Journal of Applied Behavior Analysis,* Vol. 27, pp. 401-404.

Horner, R.H., Albin, R.W., Sprague, J.R., & Todd, A.W. (1999). Positive Behavior Support. In, *Instruction of Students With Severe Disabilities* (5th ed., pp. 207-243). Upper Saddle River, NJ: Merrill-Prentice-Hall.

Jones, V. and Jones, L. (1995). *Comprehensive Classroom Management: Creating Positive Learning Environments for All Students*, 4th Edition. Needham Heights, MA: Allyn and Bacon.

Kain, C. J., Downs, J.C. & Black, D. (1988). Social Skills in the School Curriculum: A Systematic Approach. *NASSP Bulletin,* January.

Kame'enui, E.J., & Carnine, D.W. (1998). *Effective Teaching Strategies that Accommodate Diverse Learners.* Upper Saddle River, NJ: Prentice Hall.

Kerr, M.M., & Nelson, C.M. (1998). *Strategies for Managing Problem Behaviors in the Classroom* (2nd Ed.). Columbus, OH: Merrill.

Knitzer, J., Steinbery, Z., & Fleisch, B. (1990). *At the Schoolhouse Door: An Examination of Programs and Policies for Children With Behavioral and Emotional Problems.* New York: Bank Street College of Education.

Latham, G. (1998). The Birth and Death Cycles of Educational Innovations. *Principal*, Vol. 68, pp.41-43.

Lewis, T.J., Sugai, G., & Colvin, G. (1998). Reducing Problem Behavior Through a Schoolwide System of Effective Behavioral Support: Investigation of a Schoolwide Social Skills Training Program and Contextual Interventions. *School Psychology Review,* Vol. 27, pp.446-459.

Lipsey, M.W. (1992). Juvenile Delinquency Treatment: Meta-Analytic Inquiry into the Variability of Effects. In Cook et al (Eds.) *Meta-Analysis for Explanation*, pp. 83-126.

Lovitt, T. (1977). *In Spite of My Resistance, I Have Learned From Children.* Charles E. Merrill Publishing Co.

McCormack, S. (1989). Catch Them Being Good: Prevention–Not Punishment–is the Key to Effective Discipline. *Executive Educator.* January 1989, pp. 25-26.

Mayer, G.R., & Sulzer-Azeroff, B. (1990). Interventions for Vandalism. In G. Stoner, M.K. Shinn, & H.M. Walker (Eds.). *Interventions for Achievement and Behavior Problems.* Washington, D.C.: National Association of School Psychologists

Morse, W. (1982). The Place of Affective Education in Special Education. *Teaching Exceptional Children,* May.

Paine, S.C. (1984). *Structuring Your Classroom for Academic Success.* Champaign, IL: Research Press.

Payne, R.K. (1995). *A Framework: Understanding and Working with Students and Adults from Poverty.* Baytown, TX: RFT Publishing.

Peacock Hill Working Group. (1992). Problems and Promises in Special Education and Related Services for Children and Youth with Emotional or Behavioral Disorders. *Behavioral Disorders,* Vol. 16. pp. 299-313.

Phi Delta Kappa Commission on Discipline. (1982). *Handbook for Developing Schools With Good Discipline.* Bloomington, IN: Phi Delta Kappa.

Purkey, S.C., & Smith, M.S. (1983). Effective Schools: A Review. *Elementary School Journal,* Vol. 83, No. 4, pp. 427-452.

Repp, A., & Horner, R.H. (Eds.) (1999). *Functional Analysis of Problem Behavior: From Effective Assessment to Effective Support.* Belmont, CA: Wadsworth.

Rutter, M., Maughan, B., Mortimore, P., Ouston, J., and Smith, A. (1979). *Fifteen Thousand Hours: Secondary Schools and Their Effects on Children.* Cambridge, MA: Harvard University Press.

Senge, P.M. (1990). *The Fifth Discipline: The Art and Practice of the Learning Organization.* New York, NY: Doubleday.

Sprick, R. and Garrison, M. (1992). *Foundations: Establishing Positive Discipline Policies.* Longmont, CO: Sopris West, Inc.

Squires, D.A., Huitt, W.G. & Segars, J.K. (1984). *Effective Schools and Classrooms: A Research-Based Perspective.* Alexandria, VA: Association for Supervision and Curriculum Development.

Stevens, L.J., & Price, M. (1992). Meeting the Challenge of Educating Children At Risk. *Phi Delta Kappan,* Vol. 74, pp18-23.

Sugai, G., Lewis-Palmer, T., & Hagan, S. (1998). Using Functional Assessments to Develop Behavior Support Plans. *Preventing School Failure,* Vol. 43, pp. 6-13.

Sugai, G., Lewis-Palmer, T. & Hagan, S. (1998). Using Functional Assessment to Develop Behavior Support Plans. *Preventing School Failure.* Vol. 43, No. 1, pp. 6-13.

Tobin, T., Sugai, G., & Colvin, G. (1996). Patterns in Middle School Discipline Records. *Journal of Emotional and Behavioral Disorders,* Vol. 4, No. 2, pp. 82-94.

Todd, A.W., Horner, R.H., Sugai, G., & Sprague, J.R. (1999). Effective Behavior Support: Strengthening Schoolwide Systems Through a Team-based Approach. *Effective School Practices,* Vol. 17, pp. 23-37.

Wagner, M. (1991). *Drop Outs With Disabilities: What Do We Know? What Can We Do?* Menlo Park, CA: SRI International.

Walker, H.M., Colvin, G., & Ramsey, E. (1995). *Antisocial Behavior in School: Strategies and Best Practices.* Pacific Grove, CA: Brookes & Cole.

Walker, H.M., Horner, R.H., Sugai, G., Bullis, M., Spraque, J. R., Bricker, D. & Kaufman, M.J. (1996). Integrated Approaches to Preventing Antisocial Behavior Patterns Among School-age Children and Youth. *Journal of Emotional and Behavioral Disorders,* Vol. 4, pp. 193-256.

Wells, P.L. (1990). *Boys Town Education Model.* Boys Town, NE: Father Flanagan's Boys Home.

Wells, P.L. (1993). School Discipline Plans. In *Meeting the Behavioral Needs of Students.* Missouri Department of Education. Des Moines, IA: Drake University and Mountain Plains Regional Resource Center.

Wells, P.L. (1994). *Iowa Behavioral Initiative Concept Paper.* Des Moines. IA: Bureau of Special Education, Iowa Department of Education.

Wells, P.L. (1998). *Guidelines and Procedures for Student Discipline.* Leavenworth, KS: Unified School District 453, Leavenworth Public Schools.

References

Additional titles in the series
Solving the Discipline Puzzle:

Ongoing School Improvement
- Tools for Data Gathering
- Processes for Collaboration

Clarifying Expectations
How to Develop:
- Guidelines for Success
- Common Area Plans
- Classroom Procedures

Preventive Teaching
Strategies to Teach Your Behavioral Expectations

Incidental Teaching
How to Provide Feedback that Encourages & Corrects

Building Positive Relationships
Creating Bonds that Conquer Discipline Problems

To order additional copies of
Understanding Instructional Discipline
contact:

CREATING
STUDENT
SUCCESS

3748 Florentine Circle
Longmont, CO 80503
(303) 776-2083
www.creatingstudentsuccess.com